Editor in Chief
Ina Massler Levin, M.A.

Editor
Eric Migliaccio

Contributing Editor
Sarah Smith

Creative Director
Karen J. Goldfluss, M.S. Ed.

Cover Design
Tony Carrillo / Marilyn Goldberg

Teacher Created Resources, Inc.
12621 Western Avenue
Garden Grove, CA 92841
www.teachercreated.com

ISBN: 978-1-4206-5979-5

©2010 Teacher Created Resources, Inc.
Reprinted, 2018 (PO601345)

Made in U.S.A.

This book belongs to

_____

Ready·Set·Learn

Get Ready to Learn!

Get ready, get set, and go! Boost your child's learning with this exciting series of books. Geared to help children practice and master many needed skills, the *Ready·Set·Learn* books are bursting with 64 pages of learning fun. Use these books for . . .

 enrichment    skills reinforcement   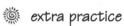 extra practice

With their smaller size, the *Ready·Set·Learn* books fit easily in children's hands, backpacks, and book bags. All your child needs to get started are pencils, crayons, and colored pencils.

A full sheet of colorful stickers is included. Use these stickers for . . .

* decorating pages

* rewarding outstanding effort

* keeping track of completed pages

Celebrate your child's progress by using these stickers on the reward chart located on the inside cover. The blue-ribbon sticker fits perfectly on the certificate on page 64.

With *Ready·Set·Learn* and a little encouragement, your child will be on the fast track to learning fun!

Match the Pairs

Directions: Trace the dashed lines to match the pairs.

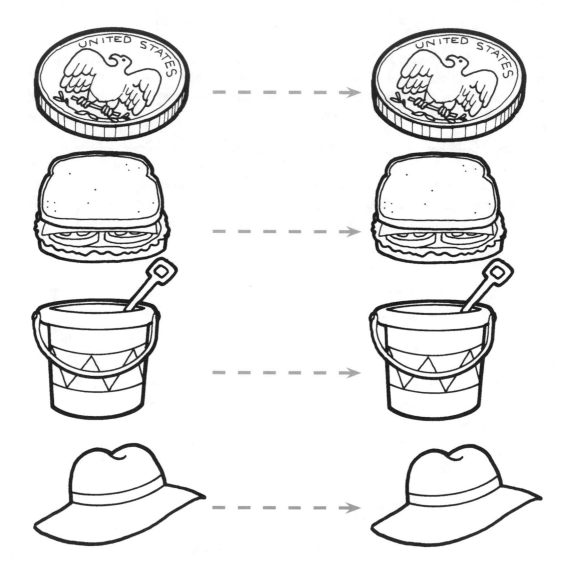

4

More Pairs

Directions: Trace the dashed lines to match the pairs.

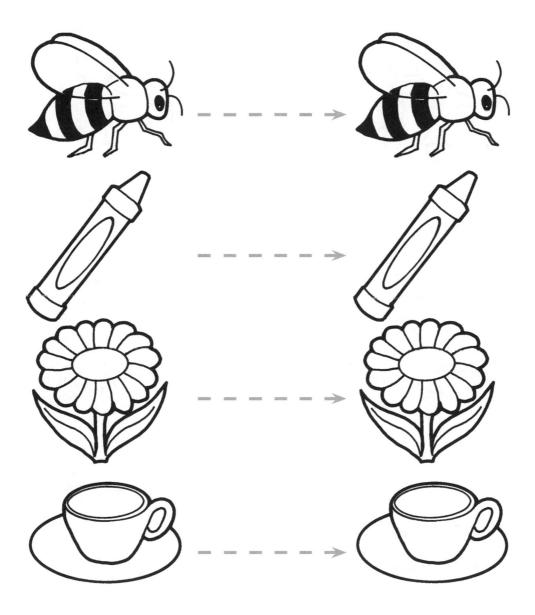

Follow the Curves

Directions: Trace the dashed lines to match the pairs.

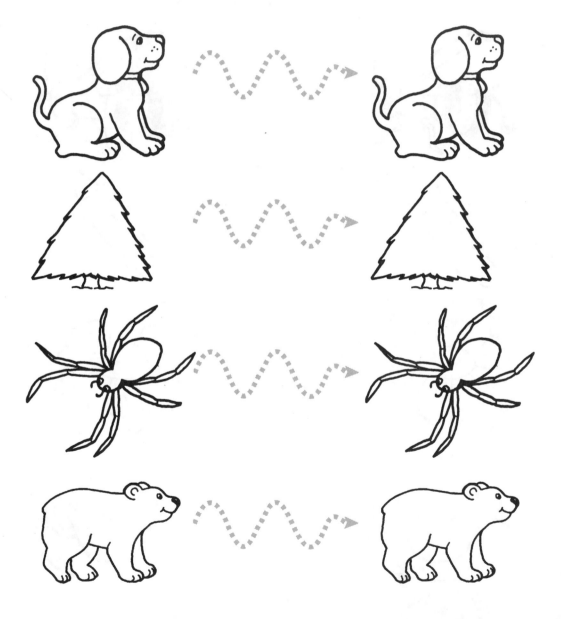

Loop the Loop

Directions: Trace the dashed lines to match the pairs.

Finish the Rocket

Directions: Finish drawing the rocket.

8

Pairs

Directions: Draw lines to match the pairs.

Partners

Directions: Draw lines to match the pairs.

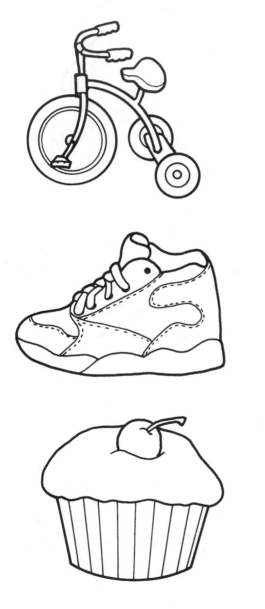

At Sea

Directions: Find and circle these things in the picture above.

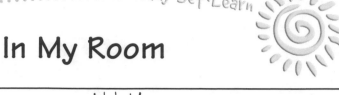

In My Room

Directions: Find and circle these things in the picture above.

Animal Search

Directions:

1. Look carefully at the audience.
2. Find and color the animals hiding among the people.

Color the Season

Directions: Color everything you might find on a sunny, spring day.

14

What Would You Wear?

Directions: Circle the pieces of clothing that you might wear on a **cold** day.

What Do You See at Night?

Directions: Color the pictures you see in the sky at night.

Hot! Don't Touch!

Directions: Look at the pictures below. Cross out the item in each row that is too hot to touch. Color the items that are safe to touch.

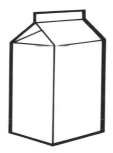

On and Off

Directions: Color the leaves that are on the tree **green** and **yellow**. Color the leaves that have fallen off the tree **orange** and **red**.

Recognizing Sizes

Directions: Circle the picture in each row that is a different size.

Finding One Larger

Directions: Look carefully at each pair of pictures. Circle the picture that is larger.

Stars of All Sizes

Directions: Circle the smallest star.

Three Bears Matching

Directions: Look at the size of each bear. Circle and color the best bowl, chair, or bed for each bear.

22

Finding Something Little

Directions: What is the smallest animal you can see in the maze? Draw a line through the maze to get to the smallest animal.

Seeing Differences

Directions: Circle the picture that is different in each row.

 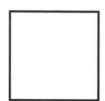 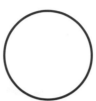 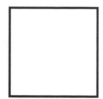

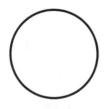 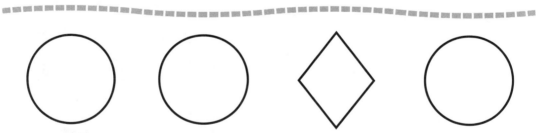  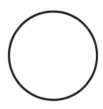

 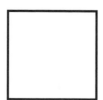 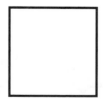 

Inside a House

Directions: Draw lines from the house to everything you might find inside it.

Inside a Barn

Directions: Draw lines from the barn to everything you might find inside it.

Swimming Buddies

Directions: Color the two fish that are the same.

Birds of a Feather

Directions: Color the two birds that are the same.

28

Can't Catch Me!

Directions: Look at the two gingerbread man cookies. Add the missing parts to the second cookie to make it the same as the first.

Where Our Things Belong

Directions: Draw lines from the things on the left to the place where they belong on the right.

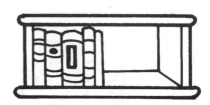

What Does Not Belong?

Directions: Color the object that does not belong.

Circle Scene

Directions: Color each item that looks like a circle.

I found ☐ circles.

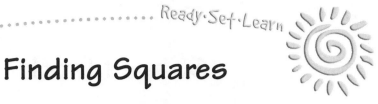

Finding Squares

Directions: All the shapes on this shirt are squares. Color all the big squares red. Color the small squares green.

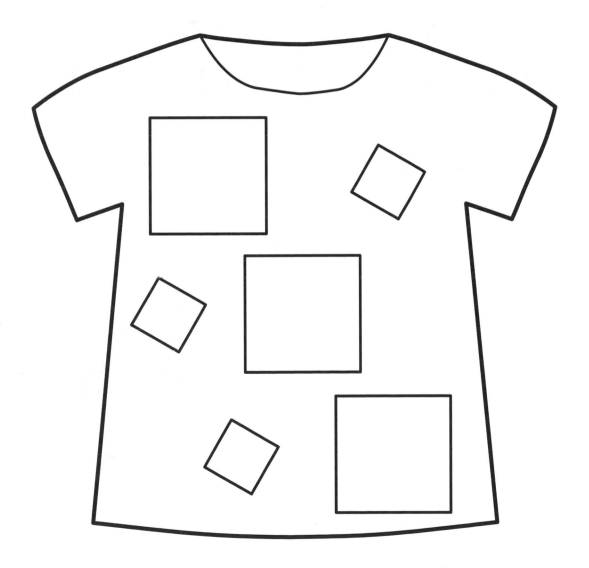

Shape Match

Directions: Name each shape and object. Draw a line from each shape to an object with the same shape.

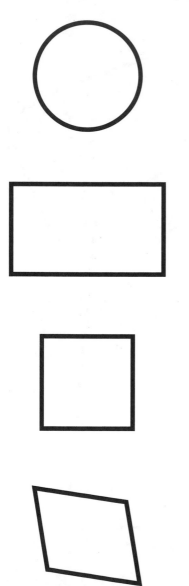

34

Hungry Hippo

Directions: Draw a line from the hungry hippo to the greater amount of food. Color the hippo and the greater amount of food.

More Monkeys

Directions: There are two groups of monkeys in each row. Circle the group that has more monkeys.

Least and Most

Directions: Compare each pair of pictures. Circle the picture that has less.

Storing Food

Directions: Count the number of acorns that each squirrel has. Count the number of acorns in each circle. Draw lines to match the number of acorns that each squirrel has with the number of acorns in each circle. Then color the pictures.

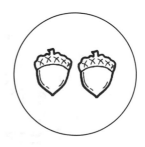

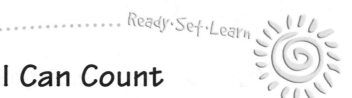

I Can Count

1. Trace your hand.

2. Color it.

3. Count your fingers.

4. Draw a line from each finger to a number.

3

2

4

1

5

Writing Numbers from 1–5

Directions: Let's practice writing numbers. Trace over the numbers below. Then write your own in the empty space.

1 1 1

2 2 2

3 3 3

4 4 4

5 5 5

How Many Children?

Directions: Count the children in each picture. Circle the correct number of children in each box.

| 4   5   8 | 3   6   2 |
| 4   1   2 | 7   6   5 |

Bubble Bath

Directions: Look at the first picture in each row. Color one of the two pictures in each row that shows the *opposite* of the first picture.

Sleep Tight

Directions: Color the picture in each row that shows the *opposite* of the picture in the first box.

awake   asleep

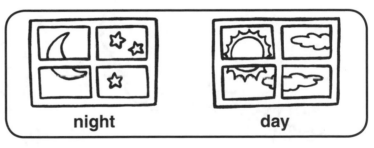

night   day

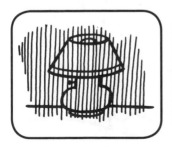

on   off

Mark the X

- Make an **X** above the tree.
- Make an **X** below the dog.
- Make an **X** on the dog's nose.

- Make an **X** inside the tree.
- Make an **X** beside the girl.
- Make an **X** under the bird.

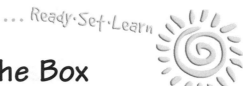

Out of the Box

Directions: Color the tools that are **out** of the box.

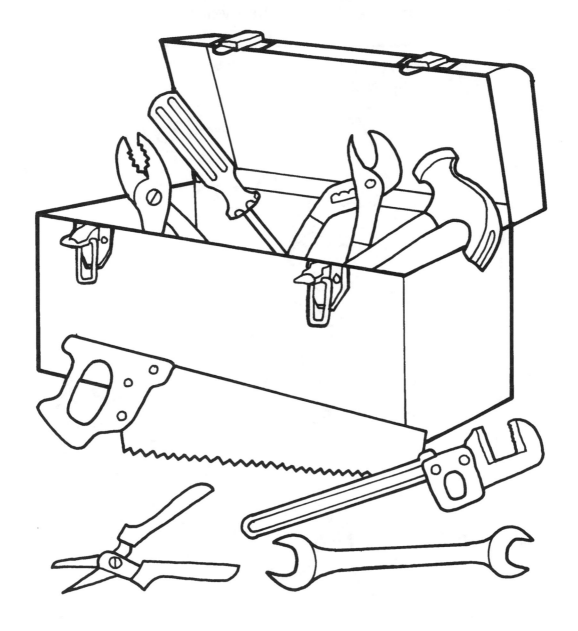

Near and Far

Directions: Color the bear that is **near** the tree brown.
Color the bear that is **far** from the tree yellow.

46

With

Directions: Color the dog that is **with** the cat.

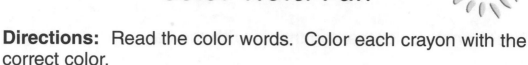

Color Word Fun

Directions: Read the color words. Color each crayon with the correct color.

red

orange

blue

black

yellow

brown

green

purple

48

A-Z

Directions: Trace the letters of the alphabet.

Aa   Bb   Cc   Dd

Ee   Ff   Gg   Hh

Ii   Jj   Kk   Ll

Mm   Nn   Oo   Pp

Qq   Rr   Ss   Tt

Uu   Vv   Ww   Xx

Yy   Zz

Uppercase Letters

Directions: Circle all of the uppercase letters.

A   r   T

w   Q   a

R   q   G

t   W   g

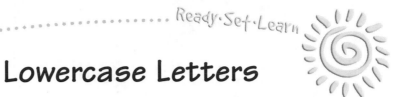

Lowercase Letters

Directions: Circle all of the lowercase letters.

Y   b   B

s   K   d

C   k   S

y   D   c

Play Ball!

Directions: Match each mitt to the ball with its partner letter. Draw a line from each uppercase letter to its lowercase partner.

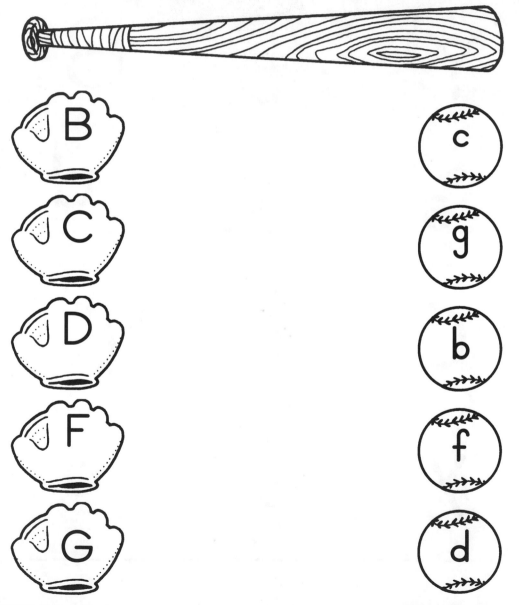

Home Sweet Home

Directions: Draw a line from each animal to its home.

Plenty of Patterns

Directions: Look at each pattern. Choose the picture in the box with the diagonal line that comes next in the pattern. Color that picture.

Gift Sequence

Directions: Write **1**, **2**, **3**, or **4** on the line in each square to show the order in which the girl wraps the gift.

A Day on the Farm

Directions: Trace the lines to find out where each animal rests.

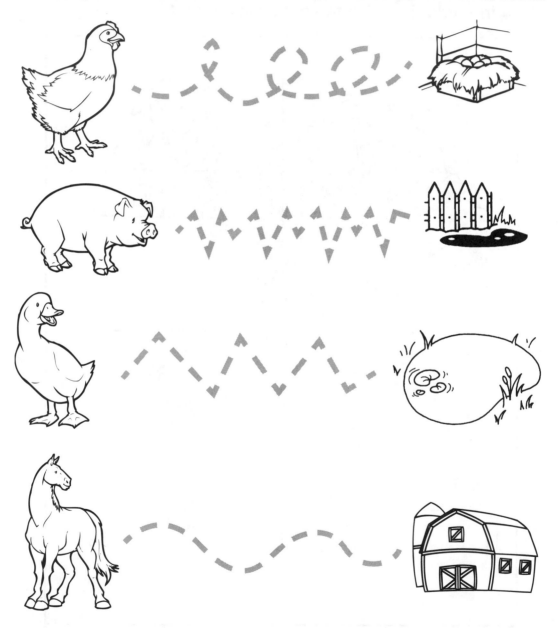

Cattle Drive

Directions: Help these cows find their way home.

Which Does Not Belong?

Directions: Look at the pictures in each row. Name each object, then circle the one that does not belong.

Before and After

Directions: Look at the three pictures in each row. Circle the word **Before** under the picture that comes before the first picture in the row. Circle the word **After** under the picture that comes after the first picture in the row.

Before   After   Before   After

Before   After   Before   After

Rhyme Time

Directions: Say the name of each picture. Draw a line to the picture that rhymes with it.

Matching Pictures

Directions: Color the pictures that are the same in the same color. Use a different color for each pair.

On the Go

Directions: Look at the vehicles on the left. Draw a line from each vehicle to the place where you would find it.

This Award
Is Presented To

_____

for

★ Doing Your Best

★ Trying Hard

★ Not Giving Up

★ Making a
  Great Effort